BENJAMIN BANNEKER

The African-American Biographies Series

MAYA ANGELOU
More Than a Poet
0-89490-684-4

LOUIS ARMSTRONG
King of Jazz
0-89490-997-5

ARTHUR ASHE
Breaking the Color Barrier
in Tennis
0-89490-689-5

BENJAMIN BANNEKER
Astronomer and Mathematician
0-7660-1208-5

RALPH BUNCHE
Winner of the Nobel Peace Prize
0-7660-1203-4

W. E. B. DU BOIS
Champion of Civil Rights
0-7660-1209-3

DUKE ELLINGTON
Giant of Jazz
0-89490-691-7

ARETHA FRANKLIN
Motown Superstar
0-89490-686-0

WHOOPI GOLDBERG
Comedian and Movie Star
0-7660-1205-0

LORRAINE HANSBERRY
Playwright and Voice of Justice
0-89490-945-2

LANGSTON HUGHES
Poet of the
Harlem Renaissance
0-89490-815-4

ZORA NEALE HURSTON
Southern Storyteller
0-89490-685-2

QUINCY JONES
Musician, Composer, Producer
0-89490-814-6

BARBARA JORDAN
Congresswoman, Lawyer,
Educator
0-89490-692-5

CORETTA SCOTT KING
Striving for
Civil Rights
0-89490-811-1

MARTIN LUTHER KING, JR.
Leader for Civil Rights
0-89490-687-9

TONI MORRISON
Nobel Prize-Winning
Author
0-89490-688-7

WALTER DEAN MYERS
Writer for Real Teens
0-7660-1206-9

JESSE OWENS
Track and Field Legend
0-89490-812-X

COLIN POWELL
Soldier and Patriot
0-89490-810-3

PAUL ROBESON
Actor, Singer,
Political Activist
0-89490-944-4

JACKIE ROBINSON
Baseball's Civil Rights
Legend
0-89490-690-9

IDA B. WELLS-BARNETT
Crusader Against Lynching
0-89490-947-9

OPRAH WINFREY
Talk Show Legend
0-7660-1207-7

CARTER G. WOODSON
Father of African-American History
0-89490-946-0

—African-American Biographies—

BENJAMIN BANNEKER

Astronomer and Mathematician

Series Consultant:
Dr. Russell L. Adams, Chairman
Department of Afro-American Studies, Howard University

Laura Baskes Litwin

Enslow Publishers, Inc.

40 Industrial Road	PO Box 38
Box 398	Aldershot
Berkeley Heights, NJ 07922	Hants GU12 6BP
USA	UK

http://www.enslow.com

Library of Congress Cataloging-in-Publication Data

Litwin, Laura Baskes.
    Benjamin Banneker : astronomer and mathematician / Laura Baskes
Litwin.
        p.   cm. — (African-American biographies)
    Includes bibliographical references and index.
    Summary: A biography of the eighteenth-century African-American who
taught himself mathematics and astronomy and helped survey what would
become Washington, D.C.
    ISBN 0-7660-1208-5
    1. Banneker, Benjamin, 1731–1806—Juvenile literature.
2. Astronomers—United States—Biography—Juvenile literature.
3. Afro-American scientists—United States—Biography—Juvenile
literature. [1. Banneker, Benjamin, 1731–1806. 2. Astronomers.
3. Afro-Americans—Biography.] I. Banneker, Benjamin, 1731–1806.
II. Title. III. Series.
QB36.B22L58   1999
520'.92–dc21
[b]   98-34913
                                               CIP
                                             AC

Printed in the United States of America

10 9 8 7 6 5 4 3 2 1

To Our Readers: All Internet addresses in this book were active and appropriate
when we went to press. Any comments or suggestions can be sent by e-mail to
Comments@enslow.com or to the address on the back cover.

Illustration Credits:
© Collection of the New-York Historical Society, p. 91; Corbis–Bettmann,
p. 45; Corbis, pp. 23, 30, 47; Frohman; Col. Louis/Corbis, p. 18; J.G.
Heck, *Iconographic Encyclopedia of Science, Literature, and Art*, N.Y.: R.
Garrigue, 1851, pp. 58, 88; Library of Congress, pp. 13, 39, 52, 65, 69,
73; Maryland Historical Society, Baltimore, pp. 55, 76, 84; Photographs
and Prints Division, Schomburg Center for Research in Black Culture,
New York Public Library, Astor, Lenox and Tilden Foundations, pp. 11,
34, 96

Cover Illustration:
Stamp Design © U.S. Postal Service. Reproduced with permission.
All rights reserved.

CONTENTS

ACKNOWLEDGMENT

The author wishes to thank Silvio A. Bedini
for reviewing the first draft of this book.

1

DESIGN FOR A
CAPITAL CITY

enjamin Banneker was leaving home for the first time in his life. Although he was fifty-nine years old, Banneker had never before traveled more than a few miles from his small tobacco farm near the Patapsco River in rural Baltimore County, Maryland.[1] It was early winter, in the year 1791, and the reason for Banneker's trip was an exciting one. Benjamin Banneker, a free black man, was going to help survey the land that would become the capital city of the young United States.

Surveyors measure an area and draw a map of its borders. In the eighteenth century, surveying could not be done without a thorough understanding of astronomy: The position of the stars was used to determine locations on the ground. Banneker had not had much formal schooling, but he was skilled in astronomy.

The Federal Territory, as the land to be surveyed was called, looked nothing like the city of Washington, D.C., today. The land that Benjamin Banneker was going to help map was still a marshy wilderness. Hidden by forest and murky swamps, it was the habitat of panthers, wild turkeys, and wolves.[2] The Powhatan and Algonquin Indian tribes had lived there too, not so very long before.

Now the new Congress of the United States needed a permanent home in a central location on the seacoast. So, in the year before, the states of Virginia and Maryland had each agreed to give up an adjoining piece of this rugged land to be used for the capital city.[3]

President George Washington, trained as a surveyor himself, chose the exact ten-mile-square area for the site. Then he chose the foremost surveyor of the time to direct the work: Major Andrew Ellicott IV.[4]

Andrew Ellicott had drawn many of the new boundary lines in the young republic. Few people shared his skills in surveying. Yet this was not a job he could do alone. Major Ellicott's cousin George Ellicott suggested that his neighbor Benjamin Banneker might make a worthy assistant.[5]

Although Andrew Ellicott had never met Benjamin Banneker, he had reviewed some of Banneker's astronomical calculations and knew he was a man with impressive scientific and mathematical abilities. Banneker had taught himself astronomy, beginning his study only two years earlier, at the age of fifty-seven, using borrowed textbooks and a borrowed telescope. He spent long nights making detailed observations of the stars. Alone, he had mastered the complex mathematical problems required to do astronomy. To have accomplished so much learning in so short a time, Banneker showed keen intelligence and great determination.

Andrew Ellicott hired Banneker as his scientific assistant for the survey, and the two men set out on horseback in early February for Alexandria, Virginia. This was the city nearest the territory they were to chart. For Banneker, who had never visited a large city before, the bustling activity on the wharves of the Alexandria seaport was strange and thrilling.[6]

At that time, great ships filled the port, bringing dry goods from England and returning with furs and tobacco from America. Sailors, merchants, travelers, and city residents filled the streets. The sweet aroma of mince pies and pumpkin bread, floating from open bakery windows, contrasted sharply with the strong odor of oysters and cod hawked by fishmongers across the street. Several taverns, or "ordinarys," as the locals called them, served tempting food and drink.[7]

The surveying team could not tarry long, however; the men had an important job to do just outside town. On a high ridge in the forest, they set up a large observation tent with a hole cut in the top for the main telescope, or zenith sector, as it was called.[8] This telescope was aimed straight up and was used to observe stars passing overhead.

As the earth rotates, stars appear above points on the earth on a predictable schedule. By knowing the exact location of the stars and the exact time of night, a surveyor can figure out the precise latitude and longitude of where he is standing. The surveyor takes many readings, then uses mathematics to compute the boundaries of the land being mapped.

Benjamin Banneker was responsible for maintaining an instrument called an astronomical clock. He closely monitored the sensitive clock's rate and temperature. Even the slightest movement or change in temperature could cause an inaccurate reading. This task required extreme concentration and diligence.

Although the cold winter months were best for stargazing, they were toughest for living in a tent. The hard ground and the frigid damp air made sleeping conditions miserable. What's more, Banneker could

This old magazine illustration shows Benjamin Banneker at work on the plans for the city of Washington, D.C. In 1791, Banneker, who had taught himself astronomy, was chosen to help survey the land for the country's future capital city.

sleep for only a few hours each afternoon. His work required long nights watching the bright stars. Such labor would have been demanding even for a man half his age. Yet Banneker did not stop working until the four straight sides of President Washington's ten-mile square had been drawn.[9]

Banneker was an able assistant to Andrew Ellicott in the survey of the Federal Territory. His careful note-taking and skill with scientific instruments helped the surveyor in this important project. That these methods were self-taught by a free black man in a time of slavery made them all the more remarkable. This was a time in which many people believed that a black man's intellect was inferior to that of a white man's. In mid-March 1791, the *Georgetown Weekly Ledger* filed this report:

> Some time last month arrived in this town Mr. Andrew Ellicot, a gentleman of superior astronomical abilities. He was employed by the President of the United States of America, to lay off a tract of land, ten miles square, on the Potowmack, for the use of Congress;—is now engaged in this business, and hopes soon to accomplish the object of his mission. He is attended by Benjamin Banniker, an Ethiopian, whose abilities, as a surveyor, and an astronomer, clearly prove that Mr. Jefferson's concluding that race of men were void of mental endowments, was without foundation.[10]

Only five months later, Benjamin Banneker would write a letter to Secretary of State Thomas Jefferson in which he would respectfully question Jefferson's views

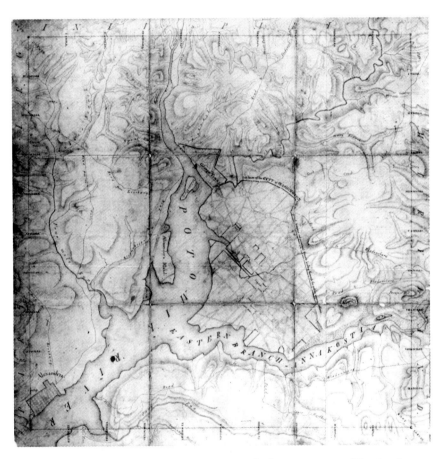

After surveying the Federal Territory with the assistance of Benjamin Banneker, Andrew Ellicott drew this map for President George Washington.

regarding race and slavery. Before the year's end, Banneker would write and have published the first of six famous almanacs and emerge as one of the country's foremost amateur astronomers. After nearly sixty years of solitude, Benjamin Banneker would spend his next decade making history.

2

A FAMILY ALBUM

enjamin Banneker was born November 9, 1731, on his family's farm in Baltimore County. His grandmother, a white woman named Molly Welsh, had an unusual background. As a girl, she had worked as a dairymaid in a small village in the English countryside. When a cow she was milking kicked over the pail, Welsh was accused of stealing the milk. In England at that time, people were hung for the crime of stealing. Welsh's life was spared because she could read.

Under a provision in the English law known as "calling for the book," prisoners who showed that they could read might have their sentence reduced. In Molly Welsh's case, she was spared the gallows, but she had to agree to go to America and work without pay for seven years.[1]

It was a treacherous voyage that brought Welsh and others to the American colonies. Greedy shipowners treated their passengers as cargo and crowded them into tiny, filthy quarters. Smallpox and other diseases carried by the packs of rats roaming onboard broke out at sea. Depending on the weather, the Atlantic crossing could take anywhere from a month and a half to more than four months. The meager rations of salted meat, ship biscuits, and water often ran out, and many passengers starved to death.[2]

Molly Welsh and her fellow travelers, among them carpenters, masons, teachers, and farmhands, reached the Maryland shore sometime in 1683. Not all the people who survived the passage were prisoners like Welsh. Carpenters and masons had come to help with all the new building in the colonies. Teachers were needed to tutor the children of the plantation owners.

Molly Welsh was purchased by a tobacco planter with a plantation near the Patapsco River.[3] For the years of her servitude, Welsh's life was like that of a slave. Her time belonged to her master; she worked from "day clean" to "first dark."[4] She ate little more every day than gruel, a thin porridge made of corn. Her clothes were stitched from rough burlap. She was required to be completely obedient to her employer at all times or risk a whipping of ten lashes. Still, the fate of a convict sent to the colonies was far better than that of a slave. After the seven years of required labor had been completed, prisoners were freed. Slaves usually remained in slavery for their whole lives.

Molly Welsh earned her freedom around the year 1690. She was in her mid-twenties, all alone and without any money. Yet this tiny, fair-skinned, blond woman bravely took scythe in hand. She managed by herself to clear some land in the nearby wilderness and plant Indian corn and tobacco. Welsh rented this land, paying off what she owed with her tobacco crops, until the day came when she was able to purchase the land outright.[5]

Once Molly Welsh owned her land, she knew that she must get some help farming it. She did not have any friends or neighbors to help her, and it was too much work for one woman. Welsh knew firsthand what it felt like to be forced from home and to be owned by another person. Yet she could not afford to pay laborers' wages, and so in 1692 she purchased two slaves.[6]

The two men who came to work on Molly Welsh's farm were very different from each other. One was strong and eager to work. He helped Welsh with the heaviest labor, including clearing trees that covered her property in the woods. He helped plow her fields and bring in the crops at the harvest.

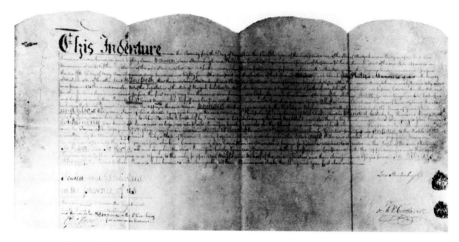

Molly Welsh, Banneker's grandmother, was shipped to America from an English prison in the late 1600s. She was forced to work without pay for seven years to earn her freedom. Many other people were sent to America under contracts like the one shown here for an indentured servant. This contract got its name from its *dented*, or scalloped, shape.

The other slave did not know very much about farmwork. He told Welsh that his name was Bannaka and that his father had been a king in his homeland.[7] It was not uncommon in Africa at that time for warring tribes to capture rivals and sell them off to European slave traders. Bannaka's claim that he was a tribal prince forced into slavery was a believable story.

Welsh's compassion for the enslaved men led her to free both of them within a few years' time. She then married Bannaka. This was a very dangerous thing for her to do. The marriage of a white woman and a black man was against the law in the colony of Maryland, where they lived.[8] Welsh and her new husband risked severe punishment. If their marriage were brought to the attention of the authorities, they would most certainly lose their land and their freedom.

Also, Welsh may not have had official papers providing evidence of her husband's freedom.[9] This was not particularly unusual, given the poor record keeping of the time. What was more unusual for the time was that Welsh owned land. In those days, women were considered the property of the men with whom they lived: first their father, and then their husband. Women had no rights of their own. If brought before a court of law, it seemed likely that Welsh's marriage, past servitude, and property would bring her trouble.

Welsh and Bannaka chose to risk a life together, apart from society. They led a simple, quiet, and hardworking existence on their remote farm in the wilderness. They did nothing to bring attention to themselves. They worked long hours cultivating tobacco, and the farm prospered. Their family prospered as well. They had four daughters, the eldest of whom was Mary, born in 1700.

Mary was a great help on the farm, especially after Bannaka died suddenly. He may have died from yellow fever, epidemics of which were common at that time.[10] Welsh and her daughter Mary were left to run the farm and take care of the younger girls.

In 1730, not very long after her father's death, Mary married a native African named Robert. While he was a slave, Robert had joined the Church of England and was baptized as Robert.[11] When he and Mary met, he had just recently been freed from slavery. Robert had no last name of his own, so he took the surname Banneky. Mary and Robert Banneky lived on the farm with Molly Welsh, helping to grow the tobacco and putting aside any money that they could save so that they might one day buy some land of their own.

For the hardworking young couple, this day came soon. Mary and Robert Banneky bought a small piece of wooded land called Timber Poynt. It was only about twenty-five acres, but it was good farmland. Timber Poynt was near enough to Molly Welsh's farm that Mary and Robert Banneky could continue to live with her while they began to work their own farm. For the

Bannekys, their new farm marked an important beginning, especially because it was at this time that their son, Benjamin, was born.

During the next years, Benjamin's parents labored to clear the forested land and plant as much tobacco, corn, and wheat as their acreage would allow. They put in a vegetable garden and some fruit trees. Their small harvests added up little by little each season, and after the sixth year's crops had been reaped and gathered, Mary and Robert Banneky had saved enough to buy a much larger farm.

Robert Banneky had kept his eye on a particular property for some time: a one-hundred-acre area called Stout. It was on high ground and had a stream running through it. It was very near both Timber Poynt and Molly Welsh's farm. On a March day in 1737, Robert Banneky paid seven thousand pounds of tobacco in exchange for the rights to Stout. He signed a contract that said that he and his son, Benjamin, who was then just six years old, would own the land together.[12]

With this contract, Robert Banneky made certain that his family's rights were protected then and in the future. When he died, the farm would become Benjamin's property. The contract ensured that no one could take away the Bannekys' land or freedom. For a former slave to become a landowner in a time of slavery was a rare accomplishment; there were few other free black landowners in those days.[13]

As soon as the land was legally his, Robert Banneky went to work. Spring was planting time, and everyone, including little Benjamin, helped out. The family planted corn and tobacco in any available space, and Banneky began clearing the land to make room for more crops. He tried to grow everything his family might need. There were few stores, and colonial farmers valued self-reliance. Banneky raised oats, rye, barley, and flax in his fields. He planted beans, cabbage, potatoes, onions, and squash in his vegetable garden.

The Bannekys worked alone. While their white neighbors helped one another with planting and harvesting, the Bannekys had to fend for themselves. As free blacks, the family was excluded from the community.[14] Many of their neighbors were slave owners who worried that their slaves would rebel if they were exposed to a free black family.

Following the fall harvest, Robert Banneky began building a house for his family. With the logs he had cut from the trees on his land, he built a one-room cabin. Banneky cut a hole for a window, but because glass was only for the wealthy, he made shutters, which could be opened and closed depending on the season. He laid the stones for a large fireplace that would be used for heating the cabin and for cooking.

With hand tools limited to an ax and a simple drill called an auger, Banneky built the furniture for the

When Banneker was born, his parents had a small tobacco farm in Maryland. Growing tobacco in the eighteenth century was very hard work. From early spring until harvest time, the labor involved was constant and grueling.

home as well. There was not much. He had no nails but fastened together a large table and stools, using wooden pegs and dowels. He built some beds, and Mary Banneky made mattresses from feathers gathered from the farm's chickens and ducks. The cabin and its contents were simple, but they were more than the family had ever known before.[15]

Mary Banneky cooked most of the family's meals in a large iron pot that hung in the fireplace. This pot was so heavy it took two people to move it. Like most of the poorer farmers in the area, the Bannekys ate a lot of hominy stew made from dried corn and other vegetables or meat. Robert Banneky hunted small game such as squirrel, hare, and raccoon, and the family ate the meat and used the skins for winter clothing. Benjamin and his father often went fishing. A good day's catch would include catfish, eel, perch, and oysters.

The farm had an orchard of fruit trees, and Mary Banneky made jams and pies of apples, pears, and plums. She collected reeds from the riverbank to make brooms and gathered bayberries to make candles. For kitchen utensils like cups and ladles, she hollowed out gourds grown in the vegetable patch.

It was also Mary Banneky's responsibility to keep herbs on hand that could be used when anyone in the family got sick. Flowers and grasses were brewed into teas to soothe fevers and sore throats. Dillweed was thought to cure hiccups. Some remedies even used mashed worms and snails. For an earache, cooked hedgehog fat was said to help if spooned into the ear. For a cut, cobwebs and leaves acted as bandages. Despite the strangeness of these cures, the country doctor of this era did not have much more to offer in the way of medicine.[16]

The Bannekys' farm animals included six cows, three pigs, two horses, and a small flock of chickens and ducks. One of Benjamin's chores was "cowpenning"—moving and fencing the livestock on a regular basis. This was done to spread the manure around to enrich the soil. Benjamin and his father also filled wheelbarrows with the rich, loamy marsh earth that ran along the river's edge. This was backbreaking labor, but it helped to improve their farm's soil.[17]

Mary and Robert Banneky were self-sufficient and diligent, and their farm succeeded. After Benjamin was born, they had three more children, all daughters: Jemima, Minta, and Molly.[18] Although the family was never prosperous, they were not hungry or wanting in any way.

The countryside the Bannekys lived in was lush. The grassy hills and deep woods were divided by the clear waters of the powerful Patapsco River. The family took pleasure in their quiet life and the beauty that surrounded them. Above all, they cherished their freedom.

3

RHYTHMS OF TIME

armers had been planting tobacco since the first days of the Europeans' arrival in the New World. It was John Rolfe—the Jamestown, Virginia, pioneer and Pocahontas's husband—who first encouraged commercial tobacco growing in the North American colonies.

The cycle of the tobacco-growing season controlled the lives of farmers like the Bannekys. From early spring through midsummer, the Bannekys planted, weeded, and kept a careful lookout for insects like cutworms, aphids, and tobacco caterpillars. By August, the leaves were ready for cutting and curing in a ventilated tobacco house. For curing, farmers hung the leaves to dry where air could circulate freely. About a month later, the tobacco was "struck," or taken down, and the stalks removed. The leaves were then tied in bundles and pressed into hogsheads, the barrels used to move and ship the tobacco.[1]

Payment for hogsheads was made in tobacco notes. A tobacco note was a piece of paper certifying the amount and type of tobacco that had been purchased by a merchant. Tobacco notes were used just like money. Robert and Mary Banneky had purchased their farms with tobacco notes.

Tobacco farming was tedious and constant work. Young Benjamin was expected to help every day with tending the crops. His main responsibility was to make certain that insects were not eating the leaves. He and his little sisters had other daily chores as well, such as picking the fruit from the farm's orchard and feeding the animals. In the winter Benjamin would go hunting and trapping with his father.[2]

It was only for a few short weeks in the winter that Benjamin could go to school. His grandmother, Molly Welsh, taught him to read and write when he was still very young. Since Welsh owed her life to her ability to read, it was of the utmost importance to her that her grandson be literate. Welsh had a treasured Bible with which Benjamin would practice his reading. He loved reading so much that a friend of his, Jacob Hall, once marveled that all Benjamin seemed to want to do was "dive into his books."[3]

Benjamin's schoolmaster instructed the neighborhood boys, both black and white, in a small one-room schoolhouse. (Girls were not sent to school until some years after the Revolutionary War.) The schoolhouse was unheated, and the children were made to sit on hard benches and keep quiet at all times. In those days, typical punishments for schoolchildren included lashings with a birch branch or being forced to stand in the corner on one leg for a long time.[4]

At school Benjamin studied arithmetic for the first time. He was good at it and liked doing mathematical puzzles. Benjamin had to stop going to school after just a few years to help run the farm, but he continued to teach himself arithmetic and to read whenever time permitted.[5] Many people in the remote rural area in which Benjamin lived could not read or write. Benjamin's family and neighbors came to him when they needed help with a letter or a calculation.[6]

In colonial America books were scarce and expensive, and Benjamin could not afford any of his own. He borrowed books first from his teacher, and later from his friends and neighbors, to extend his education. He taught himself algebra, and he read a lot about history and religion. The first printing presses in the colonies were just being established at this time in Boston, and pamphlets of religious sermons and religious poetry were the earliest texts published.

From an early age, Benjamin was interested in politics. These were the years immediately preceding the Revolutionary War, and the political climate in the colonies was exciting and constantly changing. (When the colonists finally did go to war with England, Benjamin was not permitted to fight. Military service then was limited by law to whites only.)

News of a political nature or any other kind was not easy to get. There were no newspapers in Maryland at all until Benjamin was fourteen years old. That is when the *Maryland Gazette* began publishing. Baltimore did not have a newspaper for nearly another thirty years. These first newspapers did not have much news either. Mainly, they reported the comings and goings of ships and advertised these ships' cargoes. The papers also carried notices of runaway slaves or indentured servants with rewards offered for their return.[7]

Benjamin often received what news he could from the artisans who plied their trade from farm to farm. While cobblers, blacksmiths, tinkers, and tailors had shops in Boston and Philadelphia, in the countryside they did most of their business using a horse and wagon. As the craftsmen made their way through the area, they brought with them news from the cities.

As a young man, Benjamin also was able to learn something of the world beyond the farm when he

TO BE SOLD on board the Ship *Bance-Island*, on tuesday the 6th of *May* next, at *Ashley-Ferry*, a choice cargo of about 250 fine healthy NEGROES, just arrived from the Windward & Rice Coast. —The utmost care has already been taken, and shall be continued, to keep them free from the least danger of being infected with the SMALL-POX, no boat having been on board, and all other communication with people from *Charles-Town* prevented.

Austin, Laurens, & Appleby.

N. B. Full one Half of the above Negroes have had the SMALL-POX in their own Country.

Early newspapers in the colonies did not report much news. Mostly they announced the comings and goings of ships and advertised the cargo for sale—including slaves.

traveled to nearby plantations to shop. The few stores open to the public were some distance away in Maryland towns like Joppa and Annapolis, so the larger plantation owners in the area imported what they wanted directly from England. They created what were called private storehouses. A cannon on a plantation's grounds would be fired to make it known to all that a shipment had come in. Goods included everything from clothes to farm equipment. Benjamin was able to buy what his family needed and catch up with the local news at the same time.

Except for these brief exchanges with traveling craftsmen and neighbors, Benjamin spent much of his time alone. A solitary life was common for farmers in general, but the Bannekers, as they were now called, probably felt more separate than others. Benjamin approached adulthood understanding that his fate was different. Although his family was respected by white society for their diligence, their skin color was perceived as an obstacle to real friendship.[8]

Benjamin Banneker's unusual intelligence further separated him from others. As a boy, he preferred to use his idle time not for play but for reading, creating math puzzles, or simply observing how things around him worked.

As a young man of twenty-two, Benjamin Banneker put his powers of observation to great use. At some point before this, Banneker had had an opportunity to closely examine a pocket watch. He never had a watch of his own, nor did he have a watch in his possession to copy or model when he decided to build a clock for himself.[9]

With an extraordinary ability to observe and recall, Banneker was able to reconstruct from memory the mechanisms of the pocket watch. Even though he had never before seen the inside of a clock, he enlarged the watch pieces in perfect scale. He made detailed drawings first, and then he carefully carved from wood and fashioned in brass the intricate network of gears, balances, and springs. When this maze of inner workings was finished, he added a bell, which chimed on the hour. This clock was a complicated device that appeared to have been created by an experienced clockmaker.

Word of Benjamin Banneker's wonderful striking clock spread throughout the countryside. People came from miles around to see it. It worked with precision for the rest of his life. In the mid-1700s, the average farmer did not own a watch or clock. Timepieces were expensive and, in fact, knowing the exact hour was usually not important. A farmer knew he must rise at daybreak and work until darkness. The whole notion of what time meant then was determined by the season and the chores at hand. There was rarely any time in a farmer's day to spare, although interestingly enough the phrase "killed the time" was first used in America by the tobacco planters who lived in the same region as Banneker.[10]

On the rare occasions that Benjamin Banneker had any time to kill, he was likely to bring out his flute or violin, both of which he was said to have played with some skill.[11] The mathematical puzzles he had enjoyed since his boyhood continued to bring him pleasure. Banneker and a group of others occasionally exchanged puzzles. This is one that Banneker wrote in rhyme about a wine maker and a barrel maker:

A Cooper and Vintner sat down for a talk,
Both being so groggy, that neither could walk,
Says Cooper to Vintner, "I'm the first of my trade,
There's no kind of vessel, but what I have made,
And of any shape, Sir,—just what you will,—
And of any size, Sir,—from a ton to a gill!"
"Then," says the Vintner, "you're the man for me,—
Make me a vessel, if we can agree.
The top and the bottom diameter define,
To bear that proportion as fifteen to nine;
Thirty-five inches are just what I crave,
No more and no less, in the depth, will I have;
Just thirty-nine gallons this vessel must hold,—
Then I will reward you with silver or gold,—
Give me your promise, my honest old friend?"
"I'll make it tomorrow, that you may depend!"
So the next day the Cooper his work to discharge,
Soon made the new vessel, but made it too large;—
He took out some staves, which made it too small,
And then cursed the vessel, the Vintner and all.
He beat on his breast, "By the Powers!"—he swore,

Banneker was in his early twenties when he built his famous wooden striking clock.

He never would work at his trade any more.
Now my worthy friend, find out, if you can,
The vessel's dimensions and comfort the man![12]

Six years after Banneker built the wooden striking clock, his father died. According to the terms of the deed that Robert Banneky had signed when he bought Stout, his son inherited the farm. At some time very close to this, Banneker's grandmother, Molly Welsh, died also. His sisters had each married and moved away, leaving him and his mother to manage the farm.

By this time, Banneker's mother, Mary, was in her sixties. She was described as having an "imposing" appearance with a "complexion a pale copper color, similar to that of the fairest Indian tribes, and she had an ample growth of long black hair which never became gray."[13] Though the backbreaking demands of tobacco farming had become more difficult for her, Mary still had her herb garden, which she tended carefully.[14]

Benjamin and Mary Banneker lived simply, imposing on no one. Mary made their clothes of the linen and cotton she wove herself. Banneker was once described by a neighbor as "dressed in his usual costume, a full suit of drab cloth, surmounted by a large beaver hat."[15] Tall beaver hats were very much in fashion at this time, and though relatively costly, one hat lasted a man his whole lifetime.

When Banneker was thirty-two years old, he bought

a secondhand Bible. For someone who enjoyed reading as much as he did, and who had never before owned a book, this was an important event. He celebrated his purchase with this note: "I bought this book of Honora Buchanan the 4th day of January 1763. B.B." He then noted for posterity two important dates: "Benjamin Banneker was born November the 9th, in the year of the Lord God, 1731. Robert Banneker departed this life July the 10th, 1759."[16]

The rhythm of Benjamin and Mary Banneker's life was slow and predictable. For the next dozen years, this uneventful existence persisted. What the Bannekers could not know was that after all this time, their quiet life was about to change completely.

4

NEW COMMUNITY

he Bannekers were true pioneers. The land they had cleared for their homestead was in the midst of a thick forest, far from civilization. There were other settlers in the area but not many, and none within the eye's reach. A few skirmishes with the Powhatan tribe caused some frightened settlers to relocate to the city of Baltimore.

For four decades, Benjamin Banneker endured a pioneer's lonely life. Then on a winter day in 1771, when Banneker was about forty years old, he and his mother met some new neighbors. Everything about their solitary existence was altered almost overnight.

The new neighbors were named Ellicott. Theirs was a large family of brothers, including Andrew, the well-known surveyor. The brothers had come from Pennsylvania to the Maryland wilderness to build gristmills, buildings in which grain is ground into flour or meal.

The Ellicotts had made a careful search of the colony before they settled on the place to build their mills. Since they would need water to power the machinery, they knew that they must choose a site near a river. They wanted to be near a major seaport because they intended to export their flour. The land they finally decided on was seven hundred acres on the banks of the Patapsco River.[1] Their property was less than a mile away from Benjamin Banneker's farm.

The construction of the mills began in January of 1771 and would not be finished for three years. It was extremely slow and difficult labor. All the equipment and materials had to be carried to the site on the backs of the workmen. There were no real roads in the area, so the workers had to make their way through the forest on twisting and overgrown Indian trails. The Patapsco River overflowed on a regular basis after heavy rains, making crossing it impossible. The Ellicott brothers built the first bridge to span the river.[2]

Benjamin Banneker kept a close watch on the activity going on around him. The tranquil, uninhabited valley he was used to was being transformed before his

ANDREW ELLICOTT,
Born 1754.—Died 1820,

Andrew Ellicott, a well-known surveyor, came with his brothers to the Maryland wilderness to build a mill to grind grain into flour. These new neighbors changed Benjamin Banneker's life.

eyes. The Ellicotts built homes for their extended families and a boardinghouse for their laborers. In what had been a remote area of unconnected small farms, a community was born. This new place was called Ellicott's Lower Mills. (An Upper Mills would be built later.)

Ellicott's Lower Mills was a handsome small village of quarried-stone homes with open front porches. Huge chestnut, maple, and oak trees distinguished the settlement. Horses grazed in a grassy meadow during the day and were housed for the night in a stable large enough to hold ninety of them. The brothers built a wooden sawmill a bit upstream on the river and a stone warehouse closer to the gristmills.

Two stone gristmills stood ready to produce flour. At first their purpose was a mystery to Banneker and the other farmers in the valley. Up until this time, the farmers had grown only enough wheat to feed their families. Tobacco was the only crop produced for export. The Ellicotts changed this age-old practice in one harvest. They grew fields of wheat, corn, and rye and processed the crops into flour. Their success convinced the farmers in the area that they should follow the newcomers' example. The Ellicotts' mills and a second cash crop for area farmers were established in one fell swoop.[3]

The way the mills worked was fascinating to Benjamin Banneker. He had seen other mills before, but not completely automated ones like the Ellicotts'. In theirs, machines did almost all the work. Machines unloaded the grain, emptied it onto the millstones, poured the flour into barrels, and loaded the barrels onto wagons for market. To Banneker, the workings of the automated mill were as intriguing as the workings of a striking clock.

In fact, Banneker's clock had greatly interested Joseph Ellicott, the eldest of the brothers. On a trip to England he met with a cousin named John Ellicott, who was one of the most famous clockmakers in that country. Joseph Ellicott came back to America with some clocks and tools. With the same mechanical aptitude he had used to build the gristmills, Ellicott built himself a clock.

The clock was eight feet high and had four faces. The first face marked the exact time of day and included a yearly calendar with moon phases. On the second face, the sun was painted with the planets revolving around it. The third face had a movable pointer that could be aligned with one of twenty-four different songs to be played to mark the hour. The last face was a clear pane of glass through which the viewer could observe the inner meshes of the timepiece.[4]

Joseph Ellicott's elaborate clock stood in stark contrast to Benjamin Banneker's simple wooden version, yet Banneker's achievement was evident to Ellicott. Ellicott had other clocks on which to model his own, and he had had some instruction from his clockmaker cousin. Banneker had built his clock with only a few tools and a sharp mind.

Banneker and his mother had an important role early in the mills' development. They provided the food for the mills' workers from their farm. Mary Banneker was more than seventy years old by this time, but she was still active enough that her grandsons later commented on her energy. They said that when she wanted to take some chickens to the market, "she would run them down and catch them without assistance."[5]

Once the mills' operations were established, the Ellicotts took another big step toward changing the area's economy. They opened a general store called Ellicott & Co. Ellicott & Co. was a welcoming place kept warm by Benjamin Franklin's new invention, the wood-burning stove. The store sold many things, including farm tools, gunpowder, ink, and penny candy. Its large main room was crowded with cracker barrels, grain bins, fabric bolts, and tea crates. Crockery, lanterns, and baskets hung from the rafters. Ellicott & Co. sold the first newspapers available in the region and housed the first post office as well. Before Ellicott & Co. was opened, each plantation's private storehouse had been the only available shopping, and postal service was wildly irregular.

The store was a frequent stop for most of the

valley's farmers, and Benjamin Banneker was no exception. The farmers would collect or post their mail and then gather for news and conversation. On a nice day, the men would congregate on the shop's airy second-story porch. The Revolutionary War had begun, and although very little of the fighting took place in Maryland, word of what was happening elsewhere in the colonies was of vital interest.

Though he was by nature a reserved person, Benjamin Banneker relished the time he could afford to spend in the general store. This was the first time in his life that he had a place to go and meet with others. Here for the first time Banneker enjoyed the spontaneous exchange of ideas. For someone with his agile mind, this was like the fizz being released from a shaken soda bottle. Benjamin Banneker felt he was among friends.[6]

Before the Ellicotts came to the Patapsco valley, Banneker had been a solitary figure. After they settled, things changed for him. The Ellicotts believed that all people should be treated with fairness and respect. They saw every man as equal before God. This view was taught by the religious group to which they belonged, the Society of Friends. The group had the name Friends because above all else they valued friendship, or what the Friends called "brotherly love." The Friends were also known as Quakers.

In the seventeenth century, the Friends had

migrated in great numbers from England. William Penn and his fellow Quaker emigrants founded Pennsylvania. Although at first Penn himself had slaves, very soon after the Quakers established themselves in America they taught that slavery was morally wrong and called for its end.[7] The Ellicotts never used slave labor.

The Society of Friends also believed that war was wrong, and pious Friends refused to fight in the French and Indian War and in the Revolutionary War. The Ellicotts were not so observant as this, and members of the family served in several important army posts. Andrew Ellicott IV, with whom Benjamin Banneker surveyed the capital, achieved the rank of major in the Maryland militia.

Quaker worship was different from that practiced in the other churches in the colonies. Instead of the elaborate ritual that defined the service in other churches, Quaker worship was marked by long periods of silence. The Friends believed that a person could best commune with God silently and without the help of a pastor. In a Quaker service, or meeting, as it was called, people spoke aloud only when they wanted to include others in their prayer.

Benjamin Banneker never formally joined the Society of Friends, but he was frequently in attendance at their meetings. The Ellicotts had built a Friends' Meeting House in the neighborhood, and it was here

Banneker often attended Quaker religious services, where worshipers communicate silently with God. In this illustration, the woman pointing upstairs on the left is speaking out to include others in her prayer.

that Banneker worshiped. A member of the Ellicott family described him there:

> We have seen Banneker in Elkridge Meeting house, where he always sat on the form nearest the door, his head uncovered. His ample forehead, white hair, and reverent deportment, gave him a very venerable appearance, as he leaned on the long staff (which he always carried with him) in quiet contemplation.[8]

The typical Quaker Meeting House was a simple open rectangular building with many windows to bring in the natural light. Inside, the walls were painted white and the only furniture was plain wooden benches. Men and women sat on different sides of the room, and children sat upstairs in a loft. The Friends' Meeting House reflected the simple spiritualism of the religion.

It is consistent with Benjamin Banneker's personality that he felt comfortable with the Quaker church. He himself was a peaceful man of reserve and integrity who lived simply and honestly. It is likely, too, that he was drawn to the Quakers because it was the church to which his friends the Ellicotts belonged.

Banneker's friendship with the Ellicotts played a defining role in his life. His future accomplishments would not have been possible without the encouragement and assistance of the Ellicott family. No member of this family was more instrumental in helping Banneker than George Ellicott. Only eighteen when he first met Banneker, young George Ellicott felt an

This Quaker Meeting House looks much like the one Banneker attended with his friends the Ellicotts. The conversation and mingling among friends outside the house before and after the meeting were considered as important as the service itself.

immediate accord with the much older Banneker. Both men were interested in science and in literature, and almost nothing made either man happier than time spent in deep study.

Practically from their first meeting, George Ellicott began lending Banneker books. In the few hours each day when Banneker was finished with his farming chores, he would eagerly open one of these treasured books.

Even at his young age, George Ellicott was already known as a talented amateur mathematician and astronomer. With his telescope he was able to identify the stars and was always eager to share his hobby with others. As his daughter remarked:

> He was fond of imparting instruction to every youthful inquirer after knowledge who came to his house. As early as the year 1782, during fine clear evenings of autumn, he was in the habit of giving gratuitous lessons on astronomy to any of the inhabitants of the village who wished to hear him.[9]

George Ellicott lent Banneker some astronomy textbooks, a telescope, and some surveying equipment. He then left on an extended business trip. Upon his return, Ellicott was to be very surprised at what his new friend had learned in that time.

5

NAVIGATING THE STARS

eorge Ellicott was often called away from Ellicott's Mills on business matters. He met with those involved with the mills' enterprises. He visited the company's site at the wharf in Baltimore. He surveyed roads and boundary lines. The Ellicotts' operations were thriving, and George played an important role in their success.

The new United States was prospering as well. The British had surrendered at Yorktown seven years earlier, and General George Washington was about to become the country's first president. The bald eagle had just become its national bird. A Frenchman,

Jean-Pierre-François Blanchard, the inventor of the parachute, came to America with his hot-air balloon to dazzle the crowds and join in the celebration. A hard-fought war for freedom had been won and a democracy born.

At the same time, a new world was opening for Benjamin Banneker—a whole new universe, in fact. Banneker was enthralled by his study of astronomy. It was more exciting to him than anything else he had done in his life.[1]

Banneker had lived alone since his mother's death a few years earlier. Though two of his sisters lived near-by and helped him with household chores when they could, Banneker had learned to cook and clean house for himself. He had been the sole worker on the farm for some time, but now, with his mother's former responsibilities added to his own, his hours of leisure were even fewer.

George Ellicott had lent Banneker a brass telescope with a pedestal base. In order to use it, Banneker needed a smooth and level surface. The wooden table in his cabin was the same one his father had built fifty years earlier. George Ellicott noticed that this surface was not stable enough for the telescope, and he brought a large, sturdy table from his house over to his friend's. Banneker put this oval-shaped table right next to the window.

Ellicott also supplied Banneker with drafting

instruments and four textbooks on the subject of astronomy. Two of the books had recently been written by one of the most famous astronomers of the day, a Scotsman named James Ferguson. Ferguson's books were entitled *An Easy Introduction to Astronomy* and *Astronomy Explained Upon Sir Isaac Newton's Principles and made easy for those who have not studied Mathematics.*

Ferguson's volumes were written as their titles promised, in clear and simple language that could be understood by even the beginning amateur astronomer. The books' many illustrations helped to further explain the text. Through his writings and frequent lectures, Ferguson aimed to bring an understanding of astronomy to a wide audience. He believed that the general public was capable not only of comprehending the science but also of seeing its beauty.

Ferguson's confidence in people's ability to learn things was typical of his time. In Europe and in the American colonies, the eighteenth century was hailed as an age of enlightenment. An enlightened person used reasoned thought and science to guide his life. A philosopher who lived then, Immanuel Kant, described his time as one in which the world first "dared to know." Newton's discovery of gravity and the discoveries of other laws that govern the physical universe thrilled thinkers. It suddenly seemed possible that people could understand all that had once seemed inexplicable.

In the 1700s, astronomers used telescopes and compasses to chart the sky. For Banneker, the study of astronomy was more exciting than anything else he had ever done.

Benjamin Banneker read James Ferguson's books eagerly, taking many notes. Of the other two books Ellicott had given him, Banneker turned most often to astronomer Charles Leadbetter's *A Compleat System of Astronomy*. This thorough account of the science was much more difficult to read than the Ferguson texts. The last book, *Mayer's Tables*, was written in Latin. While some English translation was included in the version Banneker read, he still had to teach himself some Latin in order to fully grasp the book's contents.[2]

Ellicott had promised to discuss the textbooks with Banneker as soon as possible. All of Banneker's spare moments were now spent with telescope in hand, and he was drawn to the sky each evening. For weeks he identified constellations, plotted the cycles of the moon, and practiced using the compass and rulers. Then, with his astronomy books as reference, he began to work on the mathematical calculations involved in predicting an eclipse of the sun.[3]

Eclipses of the sun occur when the moon in its new phase passes between the sun and the earth. The shadow of the moon falls on the earth, so the observer within the shadow sees the sun wholly or partially hidden by the moon. To calculate the occurrence of an eclipse, Banneker had to teach himself the arithmetic known as logarithms. Logarithms help in the multiplying and dividing of large numbers. Banneker then used a ruler and a compass to draw the paths he predicted the sun and the moon would take while in eclipse. This drawing is called a projection.

When Banneker completed the eclipse projection, he sent it to George Ellicott. Ellicott was astounded by what Banneker had been able to teach himself. To Ellicott, Banneker's projection demonstrated a clear understanding of advanced astronomy. Ellicott knew just how difficult the math involved was, and he was impressed by how quickly Banneker had reached such a high level of comprehension. Ellicott corrected a small error in one of the calculations and returned the drawing to Banneker with a note promising that he would pay Banneker a visit as soon as he could.[4]

While Ellicott viewed the computation mistake as insignificant, Banneker was horrified.[5] He had checked and rechecked his math and could not imagine that he had made any errors. Banneker went back to his reference books and discovered that Ferguson and Leadbetter employed different approaches. Because Banneker had used both sources in his projection, he reached a slightly skewed conclusion. Banneker wrote immediately of this discovery to George Ellicott.

Benjamin Banneker's success with the eclipse projection tempted him to consider a daring next step for a novice astronomer. He believed that now he might calculate an ephemeris for an almanac. An ephemeris is an astronomical table that tells the positions of the sun, moon, and planets for every day of the year. Daily

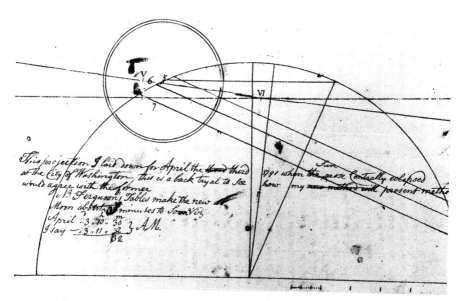

With a ruler and a compass, Banneker drew this diagram predicting a solar eclipse for the city of Washington in 1791. He had taught himself the difficult mathematics needed for the astronomical calculations.

weather predictions are made as well. Astronomers in Banneker's time figured these tables in order to have them published in almanacs.

In colonial families, only the Bible was read more frequently than the almanac. An almanac was an inexpensive standard reference book like a dictionary, providing useful information of an everyday sort. Almanac ephemerides advised farmers about the best time to plant and harvest. Mariners charted their course on the open sea by using the given positions of the stars and moon. Fishermen checked the tide schedules daily. In the many households without clocks, the almanac was used to tell time because it indicated the hours for sunrise and sunset. Almanacs were also the only calendars available, reminding readers of holidays and other important dates.[6]

Many people in colonial times believed in astrology. This pseudoscience claims that the study of the stars can reveal one's fate. Followers of astrology believe that certain days of the year are more advantageous for things like marriage, moving to a new house, planting a garden, and even taking a bath. The "lucky day" information provided in almanacs comforted those who worried that mysterious powers in the world could ruin their lives.[7]

Benjamin Franklin wrote a famous almanac, using the pen name "Richard Saunders." He published *Poor Richard's Almanack* for twenty-five years, beginning in

1732, and it was immensely popular. The witty proverbs Franklin included in every issue greatly influenced the thought of the time. When Poor Richard reminded his readers that "God helps them that help themselves" or "Lost time is never found again," he defined many of the attitudes of colonial America.[8]

Because almanacs were so popular, there were more printers who wanted to publish them than astronomers who were able to calculate the ephemerides. Typically, astronomers would prepare their calculations for a specific geographic area. A printer in Maryland, for example, would publish one almanac and a competitor in Maine would publish another. The almanacs were sold at bookshops in the cities and peddled by traveling salesmen in the countryside.

Benjamin Banneker wanted to write what was called a farmer's almanac. These books differed from others by giving more focus to agricultural issues. By the turn of the eighteenth century, more than five hundred farmer's almanacs existed. The most famous of these was called simply *The Farmer's Almanac*. It is still being published and is in wide use in the United States today.

Every night for almost a year, Banneker devoted many hours to preparing the calculations for an ephemeris. The numerous calculations involved were extremely complex, and he was careful and methodical. He copied each of the results for the three

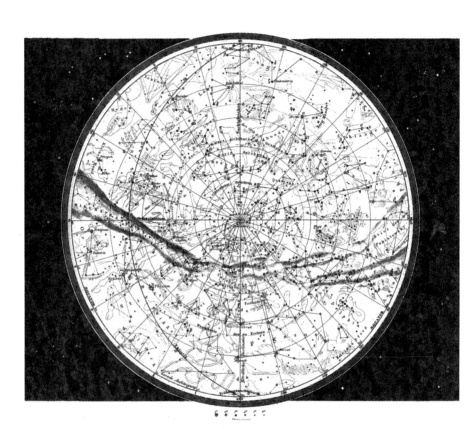

Banneker was already fifty-seven years old when he discovered astronomy. The nighttime skies filled with stars and constellations enthralled him.

hundred and sixty-five days of the coming year, 1791, into the same format used in other almanacs.

Banneker was determined not to let a single error mar his work. There were many people at this time who believed that a black man did not have the ability to figure an ephemeris. Banneker would prove these people wrong. He would show the world that a person of color was capable of great intellectual achievement.

Once it was completed, Banneker sent his ephemeris to two different printers in Baltimore. His work was immediately rejected by both men. Refusing to accept failure, Banneker sent the ephemeris to another printer, John Hayes. Hayes had been publishing the almanacs of Major Andrew Ellicott IV for some years, and so he forwarded Banneker's tables to Ellicott for his approval.[9]

When Banneker learned that Andrew Ellicott would be reviewing his work, he decided that he would plead his case directly to the major. In a letter dated May 6, 1790, Banneker wrote:

> Sir, I beg that you will not be too Severe upon me but favourable in giving your approbation as the nature of the Case will permit, knowing full well the difficulty that attends long Calculations and especially with young beginners in Astronomy, but this I know that the greater and most useful part of my Ephemeris is so near the truth that it needs but little Correction, and as to that part that may be Somewhat deficient, I hope that you will be kind enough to view with any eye of pitty as the Calculations was made more for the Sake of

gratifying the Curiosity of the public, than for any view of profit, as I suppose it to be the first attempt of the kind that ever was made in America by a person of my Complection.[10]

The letter shows that Banneker was well aware of the significance of his being the first African American to write an almanac. He knew that it was important that the almanac be published not only for the money that it might bring but also for the public acknowledgment that blacks were as intelligent as whites.

After many weeks, John Hayes made the decision not to publish the Banneker book. Hayes said that publishing Andrew Ellicott's almanacs was all that he could manage at one time. Banneker was greatly disappointed by the rejection and doubly frustrated because by the time Hayes finally got back to him, it was too late to submit his work elsewhere.[11] All the time and effort that Banneker had expended for this almanac was going to be wasted. To assemble an ephemeris for the following year, Banneker would have to redo all the calculations.

It was now December 1790. The clear winter nights were long. The stars were as bright as diamonds, and the moon was a glowing silver ball. Fifty-nine-year-old Benjamin Banneker returned to his table by the window and began again the arduous task of calculating astronomy tables. He began once more to study the sky for most of the night. After just a few hours of sleep, he would rise at dawn and put in a full day's work on his farm.

Banneker was discouraged that he had not found anyone willing to risk publishing an almanac prepared by a black man. While he contemplated what he might do next, Banneker got word of his selection to accompany Major Ellicott on the survey of the Federal Territory.

For the next three months, Banneker was involved with the design for the new capital city. Being asked to go on such a prestigious mission was an honor for him. In addition, he had never before in his life had the opportunity to leave home. Despite the hard work involved, the trip to Alexandria and the surveying area in the forest was an exciting break from the constant routine of his days and nights. When Banneker returned home from the Federal Territory, he approached his astronomy studies with renewed energy.

6

ABOLITIONISTS IN
ACTION

hen Benjamin Banneker wrote to Andrew
Ellicott IV, seeking his assistance in
promoting his ephemeris, some behind-the-
scenes efforts were set in motion. Without Banneker's
knowledge, Ellicott had forwarded the letter to a man
named James Pemberton. This single act would have
important consequences for Banneker.

James Pemberton was one of the leaders (along
with Benjamin Franklin) of a new organization called
the Pennsylvania Society for promoting the Abolition
of Slavery, the Relief of Free Negroes unlawfully held
in bondage and for Improving the Condition of the

African Race. It was more commonly referred to as the Pennsylvania Abolition Society. This group's mission was to end slavery in the United States.[1] Other states soon followed Pennsylvania's lead, and abolition societies were established in Maryland, New York, New Jersey, Rhode Island, Delaware, and Virginia.

Many of the members of the Pennsylvania Abolition Society were also members of the Society of Friends. Quakers believed that slavery was contrary to Christian values. They believed that just as they themselves did not want to be enslaved, they had no right to make slaves of others. Quakers were known for their refusal to use slave labor and for helping freed slaves start new lives, often providing them with money or land.

When Pemberton received Banneker's letter from Andrew Ellicott, he was excited. He thought that Banneker's accomplishments proved what a black person could do if given the freedom to try. Free all African Americans, the abolitionists might now argue, and there will be many more examples of black intellectual achievement.

Pemberton wrote a letter of his own to a friend in the Maryland Abolition Society, a man named Joseph Townsend. He asked Townsend to find out more about Benjamin Banneker. Townsend soon learned that two other members of the Maryland Abolition Society knew of Banneker's abilities. One was Elias Ellicott, the brother of George Ellicott. The other was John Hayes, the printer who had rejected Banneker's ephemeris. Hayes explained his reason for refusing Banneker to James Pemberton and promised to do what he could to help with publication the next year.[2]

In the meantime, Banneker had returned home from his work with the surveying team. He was worn out and glad to be back at his farm, especially because that meant he could resume his astronomy work. Despite the chilly air, Banneker had developed the habit of leaving his window seat and spending the night outdoors. One of his neighbors described him in this way:

> He mostly passed the night wrapped in his cloak and lying prostrate on the ground in contemplation of the heavenly bodies. At dawn he retired to rest, and spent a good part of the day in repose, but does not seem to have required as much sleep as ordinary mortals.[3]

Banneker had benefited from the hands-on experience he received while assisting Andrew Ellicott. For one thing, on the survey he had been able to use some of the finest astronomical instruments and texts available at that time. Most of Andrew Ellicott's equipment was made expressly for him by the foremost instrument makers in America and in England. With these powerful and sensitive telescopes, Benjamin Banneker could observe even the tiniest celestial movements.

For another, Ellicott had shown Banneker the

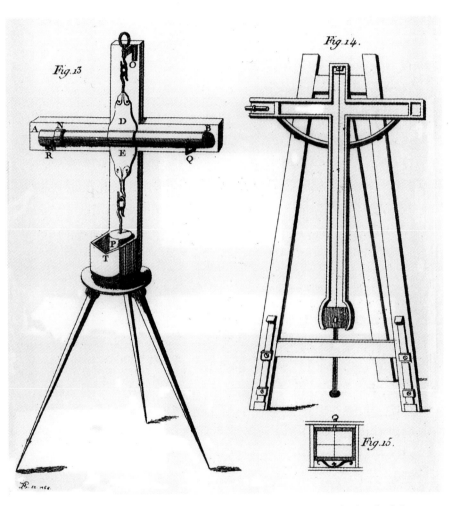

Ellicott and Banneker used levels of this type to survey the land of the Federal Territory. Andrew Ellicott had the best and most modern equipment of the time.

advantage of careful note-taking. Major Ellicott had been very strict with Banneker on this practice. To maintain the same meticulous order Ellicott had required, Banneker decided that he must keep a special journal for his observations and calculations. To this end, he purchased an elegant notebook at the general store.

Banneker had been able to squeeze in some time for his own work while on the survey. He had come back from the Federal Territory at the end of April 1791. For the next two months, he paid much more attention to astronomy than to tobacco farming. Banneker was determined to stay focused on his studies. By the beginning of June, he had filled many pages with notes and he had finished a first draft of an ephemeris for 1792.

Hoping to find an interested printer before too much time had passed, Banneker made two copies of his work and sent it to two printers. This time it was not immediately rejected. Both printers said they would consider publication. One of them, William Goddard, was a well-known publisher of newspapers and other almanacs. Banneker was pleased at the possibility of an association with Goddard, but before he made any commitment he wanted to discuss it with his trusted friend George Ellicott.

George Ellicott suggested that Banneker send a manuscript to Elias Ellicott. George's brother Elias continued to be active in both the Maryland and Pennsylvania abolition societies, and George believed that he might be of help in getting Banneker's almanac published in Philadelphia. In a city the size of Philadelphia, the almanac would get particularly wide exposure.

Elias Ellicott was eager to aid Benjamin Banneker, and he wrote to James Pemberton at once. In his letter, Ellicott stated that he knew Banneker to be a man of intelligence and integrity and that "it may be depended upon that he never had any assistance from any Person in respect to his knowledge of Astronomy."[4]

Word of Banneker's scientific skill was passing swiftly among the abolitionists. In a presentation made to the Maryland Abolition Society on the Fourth of July, Banneker was specifically named as a distinguished member of his race.[5] The path to publication of his almanac seemed to be getting smoother every day.

Still, Pemberton wanted absolute assurance of the accuracy of the ephemeris. He knew that some people would try to discredit the efforts of an African American. Before publication, he wanted to eliminate the possibility of even a trifling error. To do this, he sent Banneker's calculations to David Rittenhouse, the most respected astronomer in the entire country.

Rittenhouse counted George Washington and Benjamin Franklin among his close friends and was known for outstanding achievement in many areas of science. He reviewed Banneker's numbers as soon as he received them and told Pemberton, "I have no doubt that the Calculations are sufficiently accurate for the purposes of a common Almanac."[6]

Even with Rittenhouse's approval, Pemberton thought it best to err on the side of caution and sought the opinion of yet another master astronomer. This astronomer was William Waring, who had written an almanac of his own for five years called *Poor Will's*. Waring's review of Banneker's ephemeris was positive also, and Pemberton was now confident enough to approach a printer on Banneker's behalf.

Pemberton contacted the same publisher used by William Waring. This printer, Joseph Crukshank, was considered one of the best in Philadelphia. Crukshank was also eager to publish the achievements of African Americans. He had belonged to the Pennsylvania Abolition Society from its beginning and was a vocal opponent of slavery. He had published the poems of Phillis Wheatley, a former slave.

Three printers now had copies of Banneker's almanac in their possession. Most of the summer had come and gone by this time, yet Banneker could do little but wait. In the dark August sky, the stars of the constellations Cassiopeia, Ursa Major, Ursa Minor, Auriga, and Perseus shone brightly.

The colony of Maryland, where Banneker had grown up, was now a state in a new republic. The first

The first printed map of the Ellicott and Banneker survey of the
Federal Territory, published in 1792.

census of the United States had just been taken, with nearly four million people counted. Almost seven hundred thousand of these people were slaves.[7] Banneker was counted in a category called "other free persons," of which there were only sixty thousand.

With the encouragement of the Ellicott family, Banneker took action in support of the many of his race who were enslaved. On August 19, 1791, in a long letter to Secretary of State Thomas Jefferson, Banneker compared the situation of the slaves in America to that of the colonists under England's rule. He asked why slavery was allowed to exist in a country that had so recently fought and won its own freedom from tyranny.

Banneker cited Jefferson's famous words from the Declaration of Independence: "We hold these truths to be self-evident, that all men are created equal, and that they are endowed by their creator with certain inalienable rights." He lamented that his race was not treated as equals but instead "have long laboured under the abuse and censure of the world." He asked Jefferson to recall "this time in which you clearly saw into the injustice of a State of Slavery" and to provide "aid and assistance to our relief."[8]

Then Banneker took the bold step of confronting Jefferson personally on the slavery issue. It was true that Jefferson was a slaveholder, but he was also a

revered statesman, and few would risk offending him.
Banneker wrote:

> Sir how pitiable it is to reflect, that altho' you were so
> fully convinced of the benevolence of the Father of
> mankind, and of his equal and impartial distribution
> of those rights and privileges which He had conferred
> upon them, that you should at the Same time,
> counteract his mercies, in detaining, by fraud and
> violence, so numerous a part of my brethren, under
> groaning captivity and cruel oppression; that you
> should at the Same time, be found guilty of that most
> criminal act, which you professedly detested in others,
> with respect to yourselves.[9]

These provocative words could surely have angered
Thomas Jefferson. It is difficult to imagine that a man
of Banneker's prudent nature would have intended
this. It is more likely that Banneker was urged on by
the same abolitionists who were helping to publish his
almanac. These leaders of the antislavery movement
would have been most interested in persuading
Thomas Jefferson to support their cause.[10]

In his letter to Jefferson, Banneker enclosed a copy
of his ephemeris. On August 30, Jefferson wrote back,
thanking Banneker for his letter and agreeing with
him that slavery was unjust.

> Nobody wishes more than I do, to see such proofs as
> you exhibit that nature has given to our black brethren
> talents equal to those of the other colors of men, and
> that the appearance of a want of them is owing merely
> to the degraded condition of their existence, both in
> Africa & America. I can add, with truth, that nobody

wishes more ardently to see a good system commenced for raising the condition, both of their body & mind, to what it ought to be, as fast as the imbecility of their present existence, and other circumstances which cannot be neglected, will admit.[11]

Although Jefferson's words were inconsistent with his practice of owning slaves, his sentiments were still ones that Banneker and the abolitionists could embrace. The fact that the secretary of state professed the opinion that people of color deserved a better lot was very significant.

Jefferson ended his letter to Banneker with the news that he had sent his copy of the ephemeris to the Marquis de Condorcet in France. De Condorcet was an influential scholar and politician in his country. Jefferson meant to honor Banneker by this act. Clearly, Jefferson was impressed with Banneker's work. He wrote that he "considered it as a document to which your whole colour had a right for their justification against the doubts of which have been entertained of them."[12]

With this correspondence, Thomas Jefferson showed respect for Benjamin Banneker. The fact that Banneker had received any reply from the great statesman was exciting. That Jefferson had appeared to seriously consider the problem of slavery was a much greater distinction for Banneker.

Soon after this, the abolitionists published the set of letters in a single pamphlet, which had a large readership. Based on his correspondence with Thomas

Sir   Philadelphia Aug. 30. 1791.

I thank you sincerely for your letter of the 19th. instant
and for the Almanac it contained. no body wishes more than
I do to see such proofs as you exhibit, that nature has given
to our black brethren, talents equal to those of the other colours
of men, & that the appearance of a want of them is owing
merely to the degraded condition of their existence both in
Africa & America. I can add with truth that no body wishes
more ardently to see a good system commenced for raising the
condition both of their body & mind to what it ought to be, as
fast as the imbecillity of their present existence, and other cir-
cumstance which cannot be neglected, will admit. I have
taken the liberty of sending your almanac to Monsieur de Con-
-dorcet, Secretary of the Academy of sciences at Paris, and mem-
-ber of the Philanthropic society because I considered it as a
document to which your whole colour had a right for their
justification against the doubts which have been entertained
of them. I am with great esteem, Sir

Your most obed.t humble serv.t

Th: Jefferson

Mr. Benjamin Banneker
near Elliot's, lower mills. Baltimore count.

Secretary of State Thomas Jefferson's reply to a letter from Benjamin Banneker. Banneker wrote to Jefferson to protest the injustice of slavery.

Jefferson, Banneker would become known as one of the first African Americans to speak out against slavery. The published correspondence served both to promote the antislavery movement and to reflect its strength at the end of the eighteenth century.

The Banneker-Jefferson correspondence promoted the cause of Banneker's almanac as well. There was no question that Banneker's communication with the secretary of state would help sell his almanac. Banneker knew that a print date would have to be set soon if the ephemeris was to be useful for the coming year. He continued to await replies from the printers.

7

FAME FOR A
SHY MAN

ach time Benjamin Banneker sent his
ephemeris to a printer, he had to copy the
long and involved astronomical tables by
hand. Every copy he made took many hours to complete. With quill pen and ink, Banneker wrote in
beautiful handwriting.[1]

The abolitionists were now as anxious as Banneker
to make final the plans for publication of the almanac.
James Pemberton asked Maryland senator James
McHenry to write an introduction to it. Pemberton
believed that words from a noted statesman such as
McHenry would help distinguish the almanac.[2]

Each time he sent his work to a printer, Banneker had to copy the astronomical tables by hand. In these entries from his journal, the left-hand page shows calculations for eclipses, and the right-hand page details the positions of the planets, the times for sunrise and sunset, and the cycles of the moon.

James McHenry had been a personal assistant to George Washington during the Revolutionary War and a delegate to both the Continental and Constitutional Conventions. Now he represented the state of Maryland in the new United States Senate. McHenry assured Pemberton that he would be pleased to write a letter of introduction for his fellow Marylander Benjamin Banneker.[3]

While McHenry prepared his letter, a problem arose with the printers. William Goddard declared his intention to print an exclusive run of the almanac. Goddard said that this had been his understanding from the start and refused to allow Banneker to seek a second printing in Philadelphia.[4]

Joseph Crukshank, the Philadelphia printer, made it known that he wished as well to print the almanac. Banneker was dumbfounded. He could scarcely believe that he was now faced with the dilemma of having two printers fight over his work. Although he was thrilled with the news that his work was to be published, he worried that because he was not experienced in business, he was somehow to blame for the issue. Banneker wrote a letter to Pemberton, forwarded through Elias Ellicott, detailing his understanding of what had happened.[5]

Pemberton took matters in hand and wrote to William Goddard, seeking a compromise. Pemberton appealed to Goddard's moral sense with these words:

. . . being informed of thy attachment to the Cause of humanity, and kindly disposition towards the poor degraded Blacks . . . I now only Sollicit thy attentive benevolence to poor Banneker.[6]

Writing back a few days later, Goddard agreed to help the abolitionists' "glorious Cause" and gave his permission for the almanac to be sold in Philadelphia.[7]

In the meantime, James McHenry had delivered his introduction. It began with some of Banneker's family history and described how Banneker had taught himself astronomy. McHenry finished with a criticism of racial prejudice and slavery. He wrote:

I consider this Negro as a fresh proof that the powers of the mind are disconnected with the colour of the skin. . . . In every civilized country we shall find thousands of whites liberally educated, and who have enjoyed greater opportunities of instruction than this Negro. . . . the system that would assign to these degraded blacks an origin different from the whites . . . must be relinquished.[8]

McHenry's weighty words were an important prelude to the almanac. His association with the book was an honor for Banneker and demonstrated once again how crucial the efforts of the antislavery movement were in promoting the almanac.

Everything was now in place for publication of Benjamin Banneker's first almanac. William Goddard placed a notice in the newspaper he owned, *The Maryland Journal and Baltimore Advertiser*, which advertised "BENJAMIN BANNEKER'S highly approved ALMANACK, for 1792, to be sold by the Printer's hereof, Wholesale and Retail.[9]

There were many almanacs for 1792 about to go on sale. If Banneker worried whether the public would support an almanac written by a first-time astronomer, let alone one written by a free black man, it did not take long for his concerns to be laid to rest. The first printing of his almanac sold out almost immediately, and the publishers began to print more copies. *Benjamin Banneker's Pennsylvania, Delaware, Maryland and Virginia Almanack and Ephemeris For the Year of our Lord, 1792* was a huge success.[10]

The publishers openly advertised the fact that Banneker was African American. In a statement at the beginning of the almanac, William Goddard and his partner, James Angell, described their good fortune at being allowed to publish "what must be considered an extraordinary Effort of Genius . . . by a sable Descendant of Africa." They continued by noting "this Specimen of Ingenuity, evinces, to Demonstration, that mental Powers and Endowments are not the exclusive Excellence of white People, but that the Rays of Science may alike illumine the Minds of Men of every Clime."[11]

Goddard and Angell wanted to publicize Banneker's race for two reasons. The first was simply that they believed in the abolitionist cause and saw Banneker as a model of African-American excellence.

The second reason was that they were smart businessmen who understood that the abolitionist movement would help sell the almanac and ensure its success.

Banneker's ephemeris was the central feature of the almanac, but it was by no means the only one. Like other almanacs of the time, Banneker's included various stories and essays of general interest. One was entitled "Origin of the Gray's Mare being the Better Horse," and another called "The Two Bees."[12] Banneker did not write these stories himself, nor did he even select them. As was the custom then, the publisher of the almanac chose the works that accompanied the astronomical tables.

With the success of his almanac, Banneker's name quickly became well known. It was suddenly not unusual for him to receive guests at his cabin. Some people he knew wished to congratulate him. Others were strangers curious to see the man who had accomplished so much. Though he was a shy person, Banneker was pleased by the attention and gratified by the words of his well-wishers. He had lived and labored alone for so long. Now, at sixty, he enjoyed the change brought by his new fame.[13]

In truth, Benjamin Banneker was ready for even more change in his life. Tobacco farming had become too strenuous for him. His health had not been good for some time. He also relished the idea of having more time for astronomy.[14] If he did not need to be out in the fields all day, he would have many more hours to devote to the study of the sky. At his age, it was likely that he did not have many more years left for this.

Banneker calculated that with the small income he would receive from the sale of his almanac, he might be able to stop growing and selling tobacco. No one else depended on him for support, and he was used to a very simple way of life. Banneker decided to keep his vegetable garden and orchard so that he could grow most of the food he needed. He would rent the farmland out to neighbors.

What Banneker did not anticipate was how difficult it would be for him to act as a landlord. He simply did not have the personality for it. His tenants often forgot to pay him the rent, yet he felt uncomfortable reminding them. At other times he found himself forced to quibble over the amount of money owed. For someone who had always valued a peaceful coexistence with his neighbors, the situation was more than Banneker could bear.[15]

Banneker decided that he must sell his land. This was a very hard decision for a man who had been a farmer his whole life. The land had been bequeathed to him by his father, a proud landowner who taught his family that land ensured freedom. Yet Banneker had no children to help him or to whom he might leave the farm. He could not afford to pay others to work his land. Banneker could see no alternative to selling.[16]

As might be expected, Banneker approached the Ellicotts first. The mill owners agreed at once to buy Banneker's farm for a fair price, with the understanding that he continue to live there for as long as he wished. While the Ellicotts were known to be just in their dealings with everyone, they gave special consideration to their friend. In this business transaction, the Ellicotts made certain that Banneker was well provided for.

First, they guaranteed Banneker a constant yearly income so that he would not have to worry about his future. Banneker himself figured the breakdown of the Ellicotts' payments based on his estimate that he would live another fifteen years from the time of the sale. Second, the Ellicotts opened a credit account at their store in Banneker's name. Any purchases that Banneker charged were simply subtracted from the Ellicotts' payment to him at the end of the year.

Banneker kept a careful record of the things he bought at Ellicott & Co. His lists included everyday items like shoes (11 shillings), a padlock (2 shillings), and an inkstand (3 shillings). One entry noted the purchase of a pocket watch (4 dollars).[17]

The sale of his land and the almanac provided Banneker with the income he needed to live comfortably and spend most of his time studying. Banneker completed an ephemeris for 1793 in the next few months, and the same printers quickly agreed to publish his work again.

The second almanac included Banneker's correspondence with Thomas Jefferson. In addition, there was an essay called "A Plan for a Peace Office for the United States." Written by a well-known Quaker doctor named Benjamin Rush, the essay proposed the creation of a new cabinet position in the government. Since the United States had a secretary of war, Rush argued, why did it not also have a "Secretary of Peace" whose job it would be to "promote and preserve perpetual peace."[18]

Banneker's almanac for 1793 was an even greater triumph than his first. With an ephemeris completed by a free black man, plus the Jefferson letters and Rush essay, the almanac was heralded as an important political work. A second printing was required right away. Bookstores could not keep enough copies in stock. Banneker's almanac sold in far greater numbers than Andrew Ellicott's did for the same year.[19]

Benjamin Banneker's almanacs were published for the next four years. The 1794 edition sold more copies than any of the others. In 1795 a woodcut portrait of Banneker appeared on the front cover. One of the 1796 printings included a preface stating that "the Maker of the Universe is no respecter of colours; that the colour of the skin is no ways connected with

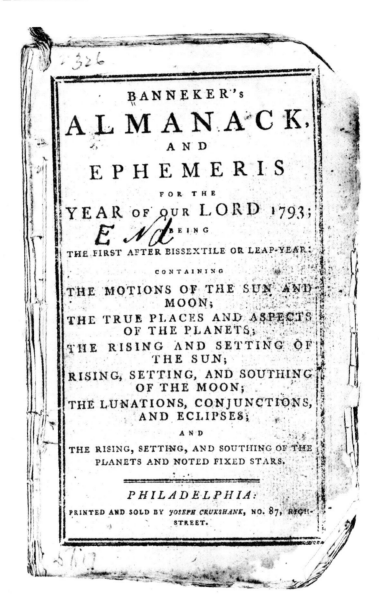

The title page to Benjamin Banneker's 1793 almanac, which also included copies of his correspondence with Thomas Jefferson. This almanac sold extremely well and was a great triumph for Banneker.

strength of mind or intellectual powers." The 1797 almanac was the last one to be published.

The astronomical journal kept by Banneker shows that he calculated ephemerides for every year through 1805. Yet he did not publish an almanac after 1797. The movement behind Banneker's publications had lost its vigor by the end of the 1790s. The early abolitionist movement in America enjoyed its heyday during the same years that Banneker's almanacs were being published. The Maryland Abolition Society closed its doors in 1797; it is no coincidence that this was also the last year that Banneker had an almanac published.

Though many Americans still believed that slavery was wrong, the founding fathers were focusing their energies on the creation of a national government. For the country to survive, they believed, the states must now act as one. Slavery was deemed a local issue, one that invariably brought with it heated argument between northern and southern states. The statesmen and politicians of the time decided it best to give the slavery issue a rest. The nation's few abolitionists had no choice but to follow suit.

8

AN HONORABLE LIFE

hen Benjamin Banneker retired from farming, he was able for the first time in his life to pursue only the projects that truly interested him. Being a man with many interests, he kept very busy. Even though he was no longer producing his ephemerides, astronomy remained his first priority, although other activities occupied his time as well.

Banneker kept bees, a hobby common to many farmers in the area. His hives had been started by his father when Banneker was a boy. Robert Banneky had maintained the hives for the honey they produced.

Ever the man of science, Benjamin Banneker was more interested in the bees themselves. The hierarchy of the colony fascinated Banneker, and he kept detailed observations of what he saw.

In addition to his astronomy journal, Banneker kept another record of more ordinary occurrences. This commonplace book, or diary, was filled with descriptions made by a naturalist. Banneker wrote entries about seventeen-year locusts, for example:

> . . . their periodical return is seventeen years: but they, like the comets, make but a short stay with us. The female has a sting in her tail as sharp and hard as a thorn, with which she perforates the branches of the trees, and in the holes lays eggs.[1]

and entries about unusual weather:

> 1803, Feb. 2d. In the morning part of the day, there arose a very dark cloud, followed by snow and hail, a flash of lightning and loud thunder crack; and then the storm abated until afternoon, when another cloud arose at the same point, viz: the north-west, with a beautiful shower of snow. But what beautified the snow was the brightness of the sun, which was near setting at the time. I looked for the rainbow, or rather snowbow, but I think the snow was of too dense a nature to exhibit the representation of the bow in the cloud.[2]

Banneker observed the natural world much as he observed the heavens. His was the perspective of a man of science who dearly loved his subject. Even as a little boy, he had delighted in the natural wonders around him. He studied the slow movement of the

After he retired from farming, Banneker at last had free time for hobbies such as beekeeping. Ever the man of science, he was more interested in the bees' behavior than in their honey.

tobacco slugs; he collected shiny rocks from the river; he pulled apart cherry blossoms to see the parts of the flower. Now, in his waning years, Banneker again had time to study the familiar beauty of his surroundings.

Benjamin Banneker never married, and he had few friends other than the Ellicott family. When he was sixty-five, he met a friend of theirs, Susanna Mason. Mason had heard the Ellicotts speak highly of Banneker, and she and her daughter paid him a visit. Her daughter recalled their meeting:

> We found the venerable star-gazer under a wide spreading pear tree, laden with delicious fruit; he came forward to meet us, and bade us welcome to his lowly dwelling. It was built of logs, one story in height, and was surrounded by an orchard. In one corner of the room was suspended a clock of his own construction, which was a true herald of departing hours. He took down from a shelf a little book, wherein he registered the names of those, by whose visits he felt particularly honored, and recorded my mother's name upon the list; he then, diffidently, but very respectfully, requested her acceptance of one of his Almanacs in manuscript.[3]

Banneker and Mason exchanged letters following this visit. She wrote a poem for Banneker, which said, in part:

> *Well pleased, I heard, ere 'twas my lot*
> *To see thee in thy humble cot.*
> *That genius smiled upon thy birth,*
> *And application called it forth.*[4]

Banneker's reply was heartfelt as well. He began his letter: "Dear Female Friend, I have thought of you every day since I saw you last, and of my promise in respect of composing some verses for your amusement. . . ." The letter continued: "I say my will is good to oblige you, if I had it in my power, because you gave me good advice, and edifying language, in that piece of poetry which you was pleased to present unto me, and I can but love and thank you for the same."[5]

It is clear that the meeting with Susanna Mason meant a great deal to Banneker. Like so many of his other new and rewarding experiences, this one came late in his life.

In the years following his retirement, Banneker was able to spend more time at the Ellicott & Co. store. A clerk who worked there in 1800 recalled Banneker's daily visits:

> After making his purchases, he usually went to the part of the store where George Ellicott was in the habit of sitting, to converse with him about the affairs of our government, and other matters. He [Banneker] seemed to be acquainted with everything of importance that was passing in the country. I recollect to have seen his almanacs in my father's house and believe they were the only ones in the neighborhood.[6]

On an October day in 1806, Benjamin Banneker returned from his regular morning walk feeling sick. At home in his log cabin, he died that same afternoon.

Benjamin Bannaker's
PENNSYLVANIA, DELAWARE, MARY-
LAND, AND VIRGINIA
A L M A N A C,
FOR THE
YEAR of our LORD 1795;
Being the Third after Leap-Year.

PHILADELPHIA:
Printed for WILLIAM GIBBONS, Cherry Street

The title page of Benjamin Banneker's Almanac (1795)
© *Collection of the New-York Historical Society*

Banneker's 1795 almanac was the first to feature his picture. The different spelling of his name was not unusual at a time when names were often spelled phonetically.

Banneker would have turned seventy-five the following month.

Banneker had arranged for the distribution of his few possessions. He asked that the astronomy texts, telescopes and other instruments, and the large oval table be returned to George Ellicott. He added to these his astronomical journal and commonplace book, both of which he knew his dear friend Ellicott would treasure. Banneker left his sisters his Bible and a feather mattress. (A few years after his death, one of Banneker's sisters reported finding a small bag of money hidden within the mattress.)[7]

Benjamin Banneker was buried beneath a tulip tree on his former property two days after he died. During the funeral, in plain view of the mourners, his log house somehow caught fire. The house and everything inside it, including Banneker's famous wooden clock, were destroyed.

A Baltimore newspaper ran an obituary, which expressed in moving terms how highly Benjamin Banneker was regarded by those who knew him. The obituary read, in part:

> He was well known in his neighborhood for his quiet and peaceable demeanor, and among scientific men as an astronomer and mathematician. . . . Mr. Banneker is a prominent instance to prove that a descendant of Africa is susceptible of as great mental improvement and deep knowledge into the mysteries of nature as that of any other nation.[8]

As the obituary noted, Benjamin Banneker was always a humble man. His success never made him a lot of money. What it did provide was enough for him to devote himself full-time to his studies. The renown that came from the publication of his almanacs pleased him, but Banneker never lost sight of the fact that he had not succeeded alone. Banneker knew that without the assistance of the Ellicott family and other abolitionists like James Pemberton, his fate might have been very different.

About thirty years after his death, George Ellicott's daughter Martha began work on a biography of Banneker. Martha Ellicott was only a girl when Banneker died, but she grew up hearing her family tell many stories about him. Martha married a man named Nathan Tyson, who was, like her, a Quaker and a member of a prominent abolitionist family. The Tysons had twelve children, but somehow Martha was able to sneak in some hours between child rearing to write what she called her "Sketch" of Benjamin Banneker.

Much of what we know today about Banneker comes from this short biography. Martha Tyson understood the importance of his legacy and wanted to make certain that the world would not forget him. She believed that he played an important part in American history and wrote:

> He appears to have been the pioneer in the movement in this part of the world, toward the improvement of

his race; at a period of our history when the negro occupied almost the lowest possible grade in the scale of human beings, Banneker had struck out for himself a course, hitherto untraveled by men of his class, and had already earned himself a respectable position amongst men of science.[9]

In 1954, almost one hundred fifty years after Benjamin Banneker died, the Maryland Historical Sites Commission placed a marker near the former site of Banneker's farm. Where Banneker lived is now a street called Oella Avenue, between the towns of Catonsville and Oella, Maryland. The marker reads:

BENJAMIN BANNEKER
(1731–1806)
THE SELF-EDUCATED NEGRO
MATHEMATICIAN AND ASTRONOMER
WAS BORN, LIVED HIS ENTIRE LIFE
AND DIED NEAR HERE.
HE ASSISTED IN SURVEYING THE
DISTRICT OF COLUMBIA, 1791, AND
PUBLISHED THE FIRST MARYLAND
ALMANAC, 1792. THOMAS JEFFERSON
RECOGNIZED HIS ACHIEVEMENTS.[10]

Today, there is a new Benjamin Banneker Historical Park and Museum. The exact location of the Banneker homestead was determined by archaeological digs done in the 1980s. There are plans to reconstruct the homestead to look just as it did in Banneker's time. Visitors to the park can also see George Ellicott's restored home near the Patapsco

River. The region today looks very different from the way it looked when Banneker and Ellicott lived there. Modern buildings and highways have replaced the log houses and twisting Indian trails. What was wilderness two hundred years ago is now a suburb of Baltimore.

It is in the Baltimore area that the story of Benjamin Banneker is told most often. The people of Baltimore County are proud of their native son. Schools and other sites are named after Banneker, and a museum is devoted to his life and work. Yet the life of Benjamin Banneker is more than a Maryland story; it is an American story. Banneker was a great American man of science. His place in history is as important for what it teaches about science as for what it teaches about overcoming prejudice.

Banneker lived in a time when African Americans were considered by many to be an inferior race, and he had none of the advantages of education. Yet he was as good a man of science as many of the astronomers of his time. The astronomical calculations that he taught himself were exceedingly complicated. His scientific achievements were outstanding for any person of any color.

Benjamin Banneker's life dispels another prejudice as well: that of age. Banneker showed the world that it is never too late to learn. He was fifty-seven years old when he first handled a telescope. He was fifty-nine years old when he took part in the survey of our

Today, Banneker is remembered both as a man of science and as a voice for his people, one of the first African Americans to speak out against slavery.

nation's capital. He was sixty when his first almanac was published.

Benjamin Banneker also played a quiet role in the antislavery movement. He was a modest and careful man who disliked any sort of confrontation. In addition, as a free black in a time of slavery, he had always avoided unwanted attention. Still, with the support of the abolitionists, Banneker wrote his now-famous letter to Thomas Jefferson. Banneker's was most certainly one of the earliest and most eloquent African-American expressions against slavery, though he might not have risked offending Jefferson without strong prompting from others.

Banneker was held up as an example of African-American intellectual equality in exchange for the abolitionists' assistance in promoting his almanacs. Banneker and the abolitionists helped one another to achieve their goals.

Benjamin Banneker and George Ellicott's relationship was of a different sort; theirs was a truly devoted friendship. Banneker's almanac for 1794 included the opinion "We must think well of that man, who uses his best endeavours to associate with none but virtuous friends." Despite the difference in their age and color, Banneker and Ellicott shared a love of science, a belief in the value of lifelong study, and a deep respect for each other.

Without the Ellicott family, Benjamin Banneker's

life story would have been quite different. This honorable Quaker family did more to encourage and assist him in his pursuit of scientific excellence than anyone else. What's more, the Ellicotts opened doors for Banneker to a society that had always been closed to him.

It is hard to imagine what it must have been like to live as a free black in colonial America. Benjamin Banneker was not a slave, but he was not welcome in white society. He was a man between worlds, a man without peers. For the first half of his life, Banneker lived completely isolated from the outside world, associating with no one but his family. For forty years, Banneker had no one with whom to share his interests.

Then, in his last two decades, Banneker completed what might have been a lifetime of work for another man. This self-taught mathematician and astronomer published six almanacs, assisted in the survey of the Federal Territory, and corresponded with Thomas Jefferson. Against long odds, Benjamin Banneker left a distinguished mark in the history of our country.

CHRONOLOGY

1731—Benjamin Banneker is born on November 9 to Mary and Robert Banneky.

1737—The Banneker family purchases a hundred-acre tobacco farm outside Baltimore.

1753—Banneker builds a celebrated wooden clock.

1759—Banneker's father dies and Banneker inherits the family homestead.

1763—Banneker buys his first book, a secondhand Bible.

1771—The Ellicott family moves into the region and builds two gristmills, transforming the economy of the valley.

1789—Banneker begins teaching himself astronomy.

1791—Banneker helps survey what will become the capital of the United States; Banneker and Thomas Jefferson correspond on the subject of slavery.

1792—Banneker publishes his first almanac.

1793—Banneker publishes his second almanac.

1797—Banneker publishes his sixth and final almanac.

1806—Benjamin Banneker dies on October 9, exactly one month before his seventy-fifth birthday.

Chapter Notes

Chapter 1. Design for a Capital City

1. Martha E. Tyson, *A Sketch of the Life of Benjamin Banneker, From Notes Taken in 1836* (Baltimore: John D. Toy, 1854), pp. 11–12.

2. Ibid, p. 6.

3. John W. Reps, *Washington on View, The Nation's Capital Since 1790* (Chapel Hill: University of North Carolina Press, 1991), p. 12.

4. Letter from Thomas Jefferson to Andrew Ellicott dated February 2, 1791 (Library of Congress, Manuscript Division, Thomas Jefferson papers).

5. Silvio A. Bedini, *The Life of Benjamin Banneker* (New York: Charles Scribner's Sons, 1972), p. 108.

6. Ibid., pp. 111–112.

7. David Hackett Fischer, *Albion's Seed: Four British Folkways in America* (New York: Oxford University Press, 1989), p. 257.

8. Bedini, pp. 112–113.

9. Ibid., pp. 125–126.

10. *The Georgetown Weekly Ledger*, March 12, 1791, reprinted in Richard W. Stephenson, *A Plan Wholly New: Pierre Charles L'Enfant's Plan of the City of Washington* (Library of Congress, 1993), p. 19.

Chapter 2. A Family Album

1. Silvio A. Bedini, *The Life of Benjamin Banneker* (New York: Charles Scribner's Sons, 1972), pp. 9–10.

2. David Hackett Fischer, *Albion's Seed: Four British Folkways in America* (New York: Oxford University Press, 1989), p. 421.

3. Bedini, p. 13.

4. Fischer, p. 373.

5. Martha E. Tyson, *Banneker, the Afric-American Astronomer. From the Posthumous Papers of Martha E. Tyson. Edited by her Daughter* (Philadelphia: Friends' Book Association, 1884), p. 9.

6. Ibid., p. 10.

7. Ibid.

8. Bedini, pp. 18–19.

9. Ibid., pp. 19–20.

10. Fischer, p. 52.

11. Bedini, p. 23.

12. John H. B. Latrobe, "Memoir of Benjamin Banneker, Read Before the Maryland Historical Society," *Maryland Colonization Journal*, May 1845, p. 6.

13. Personal interview with Silvio A. Bedini, September 19, 1997.

14. Bedini, p. 30.

15. Ibid., p. 31.

16. Elizabeth George Speare, *Life in Colonial America* (New York: Random House, 1963), pp. 77–78.

17. Bedini., p. 38.

18. Note to the author from Silvio Bedini, May 25, 1998.

Chapter 3. Rhythms of Time

1. Joseph C. Robert, *The Story of Tobacco in America* (New York: Alfred A. Knopf, 1952), pp. 17–18.

2. Silvio A. Bedini, *The Life of Benjamin Banneker* (New York: Charles Scribner's Sons, 1972), pp. 32, 34.

3. Martha E. Tyson, *A Sketch of the Life of Benjamin Banneker, From Notes Taken in 1836* (Baltimore: John D. Toy, 1854), p. 5.

4. Elizabeth George Speare, *Life in Colonial America* (New York: Random House, 1963), p. 10.

5. Tyson, *Sketch*, p. 5.

6. Bedini, p. 48.

7. Speare, p. 131.

8. Bedini, p. 48.

9. Tyson, *Sketch*, pp. 9–10.

10. David Hackett Fischer, *Albion's Seed: Four British Folkways in America* (New York: Oxford University Press, 1989), p. 373.

11. Bedini, p. 47.

12. Tyson, *Sketch*, p. 20.

13. Martha E. Tyson, *Banneker, the Afric-American Astronomer. From the Posthumous Papers of Martha E. Tyson. Edited by Her Daughter* (Philadelphia: Friends' Book Association, 1884), p. 25.

14. Ibid.

15. Tyson, *Sketch*, p. 12.

16. Tyson, *Banneker*, p. 12.

Chapter 4. New Community

1. Silvio A. Bedini, *The Life of Benjamin Banneker* (New York: Charles Scribner's Sons, 1972), pp. 51–52.

2. Ibid., pp. 52–57.

3. Martha E. Tyson, *A Sketch of the Life of Benjamin Banneker, From Notes Taken in 1836* (Baltimore: John D. Toy, 1854), p. 6.

4. Bedini, p. 71.

5. Martha E. Tyson, *Banneker, the Afric-American Astronomer. From the Posthumous Papers of Martha E. Tyson. Edited by Her Daughter* (Philadelphia: Friends' Book Association, 1884), p. 25.

6. Bedini, p. 72.

7. David Hackett Fischer, *Albion's Seed: Four British Folkways in America* (New York: Oxford University Press, 1989), p. 601.

8. Tyson, *Sketch*, p. 14.

9. Martha E. Tyson, *Settlement of Ellicott's Mills, With Fragments of History herewith Connected, Written at the Request of Evan T. Ellicott* (Baltimore: Maryland Historical Society, 1871), p. 47; cited in Bedini, p. 74.

Chapter 5. Navigating the Stars

1. Silvio A. Bedini, *The Life of Benjamin Banneker* (New York: Charles Scribner's Sons, 1972), p. 81.

2. Martha E. Tyson, *Banneker, the Afric-American Astronomer. From the Posthumous Papers of Martha E. Tyson. Edited by Her Daughter* (Philadelphia: Friends' Book Association, 1884), p. 71.

3. Bedini, p. 80.

4. Ibid., p. 81.

5. Personal interview with Silvio A. Bedini, September 19, 1997.

6. Robb Sagendorph, *America and Her Almanacs: Wit, Wisdom & Weather, 1639–1970* (Dublin, N.H.: Yankee Inc., 1970), p. 17.

7. Ibid., pp. 55–59.

8. Ibid., p. 76.

9. Bedini, p. 91.

10. Letter from Benjamin Banneker to Andrew Ellicott dated May 6, 1790, Pennsylvania Abolition Society Manuscripts, vol. 2 (Philadelphia: Historical Society of Pennsylvania), p. 145.

11. Bedini, p. 94.

Chapter 6. Abolitionists in Action

1. David Brion Davis, *The Problem of Slavery in the Age of Revolution 1770–1823* (Ithaca, N.Y.: Cornell University Press, 1975), pp. 216, 410.

2. Silvio A. Bedini, *The Life of Benjamin Banneker* (New York: Charles Scribner's Sons, 1972), pp. 101–102.

3. Martha E. Tyson, *Banneker, the Afric-American Astronomer. From the Posthumous Papers of Martha E. Tyson. Edited by Her Daughter* (Philadelphia: Friends' Book Association, 1884), p. 34.

4. Letter from Elias Ellicott to James Pemberton dated June 10, 1791, Pennsylvania Abolition Society Manuscripts, vol. 3 (Philadelphia: Historical Society of Pennsylvania), p. 5.

5. William Frederick Poole, *Anti-Slavery Opinions Before the Year 1800* (Cincinnati: Robert Clarke & Co., 1873), p. 10.

6. Letter from David Rittenhouse to James Pemberton dated August 6, 1791, Pennsylvania Abolition Society Manuscripts, vol. 3 (Philadelphia: Historical Society of Pennsylvania), p. 81.

7. 1790 census information on the Internet at <http://fisher.lib.virginia.edu/cgilocal/censusbin/census/cen.pl> (October 28, 1998).

8. Letter from Benjamin Banneker to Thomas Jefferson dated August 19, 1791 (Massachusetts Historical Society, Manuscripts Division).

9. Ibid.

10. Personal interview with Silvio A. Bedini, September 19, 1997.

11. Letter from Thomas Jefferson to Benjamin Banneker dated August 30, 1791 (Library of Congress, Manuscripts Division, Thomas Jefferson Papers).

12. Ibid.

Chapter 7. Fame for a Shy Man

1. Personal interview with Silvio A. Bedini, September 19, 1997.

2. Silvio A. Bedini, *The Life of Benjamin Banneker* (New York: Charles Scribner's Sons, 1972), p. 162.

3. Ibid., p. 163.

4. Letter from Elias Ellicott to James Pemberton dated August 31, 1791, Pennsylvania Abolition Society Manuscripts, vol. 3 (Philadelphia: Historical Society of Pennsylvania), p. 93.

5. Letter from Benjamin Banneker to James Pemberton dated September 3, 1791, Pennsylvania Abolition Society Manuscripts, vol. 3 (Philadelphia: Historical Society of Pennsylvania), p. 95.

6. Letter from James Pemberton to William Goddard dated September 9, 1791, Pennsylvania Abolition Society Manuscripts, vol. 3 (Philadelphia: Historical Society of Pennsylvania), p. 103.

7. Letter from William Goddard to James Pemberton dated September 13, 1791, Pennsylvania Abolition Society Manuscripts, vol. 3 (Philadelphia: Historical Society of Pennsylvania), p. 101.

8. Letter from James McHenry to Messrs. Goddard and Angell dated August 20, 1791, in *Benjamin Banneker's Pennsylvania, Delaware, Maryland, and Virginia Almanack and*

Ephemeris for the Year of our Lord, 1792 (Baltimore: William Goddard and James Angell, 1791).

9. *The Maryland Journal and Baltimore Advertiser,* December 21, 1791, reprinted in Bedini, p. 174.

10. Bedini, p. 182.

11. *Benjamin Banneker's Pennsylvania, Delaware, Maryland and Virginia Almanack and Ephemeris for the Year of our Lord, 1792* (Baltimore: William Goddard and James Angell, 1791).

12. Ibid.

13. Bedini, p. 182.

14. Ibid., p. 251.

15. Ibid., p. 238.

16. Martha E. Tyson, *Banneker, the Afric-American Astronomer. From the Posthumous Papers of Martha E. Tyson. Edited by Her Daughter* (Philadelphia: Friends' Book Association, 1884), p. 33.

17. Bedini, pp. 245–246.

18. Dr. Benjamin Rush, "A Plan for a Peace Office for the United States," *Benjamin Banneker's Pennsylvania, Delaware, Maryland and Virginia Almanack and Ephemeris, For the Year of our Lord 1793* (Baltimore: William Goddard and James Angell, 1792).

19. Bedini, p. 188.

Chapter 8. An Honorable Life

1. John H. B. Latrobe, "Memoir of Benjamin Banneker, Read Before the Maryland Historical Society," *Maryland Colonization Journal,* May 1845, p. 12.

2. Ibid.

3. Martha E. Tyson, *A Sketch of the Life of Benjamin Banneker, From Notes Taken in 1836* (Baltimore: John D. Toy, 1854), p. 14.

4. Ibid., p. 15.

5. Ibid., p. 16.

6. Martha E. Tyson, *Banneker, the Afric-American Astronomer. From the Posthumous Papers of Martha E. Tyson. Edited by Her Daughter* (Philadelphia: Friends' Book Association, 1884), pp. 53–54.

7. Tyson, *Sketch*, p. 18.

8. *The Federal Gazette and Baltimore Daily Advertiser*, October 28, 1806, reprinted in Bedini, p. 271.

9. Tyson, *Sketch*, p. 7.

10. Silvio A. Bedini, *The Life of Benjamin Banneker* (New York: Charles Scribner's Sons, 1972), p. 342.

FURTHER READING

Bedini, Silvio A. *The Life of Benjamin Banneker.* New York: Charles Scribner's Sons, 1972. 2nd edition, Maryland Historical Society, 1998.

Clark, Margaret Goff. *Benjamin Banneker: Astronomer and Scientist.* Champaign, Ill.: Garrard, 1971.

Conley, Kevin. *Benjamin Banneker, Scientist and Mathematician.* New York: Chelsea House Publishers, 1989.

Ferris, Jeri. *What Are You Figuring Now? A Story About Benjamin Banneker.* Minneapolis: Carolrhoda Books, Inc., 1988.

Patterson, Lillie. *Benjamin Banneker, Genius of Early America.* Nashville: Abingdon Press, 1978.

Schaun, George, and Virginia Schaun. *Everyday Life in Colonial Maryland.* Maryland Historical Press, 1982.

Speare, Elizabeth George. *Life in Colonial America.* New York: Random House, 1963.

INTERNET ADDRESSES

The Benjamin Banneker Story. What Is Fact and What Is Legend?

<http://research.umbc.edu/~viancour/banneker/bannekerfacts.html>

Documenting the African-American Experience. Copy of a letter from Benjamin Banneker to Thomas Jefferson, secretary of state, with his answer.

    <http://www.lib.virginia.edu/etext/readex/
      24073.html>

The Faces of Science: African Americans in the Sciences

    <http://www.lib.lsu.edu/lib/chem/display/
      banneker.html>

INDEX